# Filogra
An introduct

# Douglas K. Dix

colour photography by John Warren  line drawings by Mary French

**a Pan original** Pan Books Ltd London and Sydney

# FILOGRAPHY
an introduction to
thread sculpture

Also available in this series

Framing
Pottery
Macramé
Rugmaking
Weaving
Jewellery
Candlemaking
Crochet
Appliqué
Soft Toys
More Soft Toys
Country Crafts
Bargello

745.5

First published 1975 by Pan Books Ltd,
Cavaye Place, London SW10 9PG
ISBN 0 330 24155 9
© Douglas K. Dix 1975

Printed in Great Britain by Cripplegate Printing Co. Ltd., Edenbridge.

*2nd Printing 1975*

# Contents

Dedicated to Bert Piper, without
whose encouragement this book would
not have been completed

# Introduction

Filography is a new art form which can be enjoyed by everyone, novice or expert, children as well as adults. The materials can be picked up for only a few pence, and the designs are as individual and exciting as your own imagination can make them. Besides constructing different designs, similar ones can be adapted by using different colours, three dimensions and various materials. The patterns range from a simple design, such as the vintage car or pennyfarthing bicycle (*see* p 60), to the most complicated, Elizabeth of Hungary's crown (*see* p 54).

However ambitious you may be, I suggest you start with a fairly simple design, and progress to the more complicated. There are not many pitfalls, but those which exist will be described in detail so you can avoid my early mistakes. This is a craft, and bad workmanship will only be regretted later.

You might find these instructions rather involved at first, but do not worry; it is rather like reading instructions on how to fry an egg if you have never used a frying pan – once you have constructed one design you will probably not have to refer to the instruction chapter again.

The designs in this book fall into three main categories: circle designs, abstracts and objects. You will notice that the circle and the abstract improve as the number of nails and threads to the inch increases, and the third-dimension effect which you can obtain from spot lighting is most attractive. On the other hand, objects seem more realistic if kept simple and straightforward.

Great care must be taken when one set of threads is superimposed on another set (such as the sails of the sailing boat (*see* p 48), and Elizabeth's crown) to ensure that where the second layer weaves through the first row of nails, the threads are kept perfectly regular. One thread out of a hundred, if only 3 mm ($\frac{1}{8}$ in) out of line, shows up unmistakably and, naturally, one nail a fraction out has the same effect.

Whether you construct a filographic design just for your own pleasure, or with the aim of selling it, neatness and cleanliness at all times are essential. I have seen boards being sold in London for around £40 – but remember, one nail out of position and you would be lucky to get £4 for your design. Some of my basic designs were obtained from various projects seen along the Embankment in London, and given to me by friends, but the enjoyment of this hobby is to make up original designs yourself: there must be hundreds of other patterns possible. On average, each board takes a weekend from start to finish, but the design can take weeks of doodling.

I hope that this book will stimulate you to construct your own designs, and should be most interested to see photographs of them: do please send them to me (with a stamped, addressed envelope if you want them returned), c/o Pan Books Ltd, Cavaye Place, London SW10 9PG.

Douglas K. Dix, 1975

# Materials and equipment

The materials you require are simple and inexpensive.

**Board.** Should be at least 1.25 cm (½ in) thick when using short nails, and must not warp. Five to seven ply is ideal. When using 5 cm (2 in) nails, as in many of the circle designs, five eighths ply is correct. The supplier will cut to size, so a light rubbing with fine sandpaper is normally all you need to do. Avoid blockboard or chipboard as the odd nail can work loose, which could spoil the whole design.

**Nails.** For the flat designs 1.25 cm (½ in) panel or veneer pins should be used. Buy by weight at any good ironmonger (purchasing a couple of ounces in little plastic bags is the most expensive way). Six millimetres (¼ in) of each nail should be left showing when you have hammered it into the board. For the circle designs 4 or 5 cm (1½ or 2 in) nails, preferably with fancy heads, are used. With these, 1.25 cm (½ in) is hammered into the board.

**Accessories.** A fairly heavy hammer. Long, pointed pliers for holding each nail in position ready for the first tap. Small wire snippers if using wire. A bradawl for marking the nail positions through the paper design. Some people find it useful to have a heavy metal strip 6 mm (¼ in) thick and about 23 cm (9 in) long to check the height of the nails when hammering a long row.

**Drawing instruments.** A collection of rulers showing various divisions, centimetres and inches. Two circular plastic protractors, one 13 cm (5 in) in diameter, and the other 10 cm (4 in). A good supply of pencils.

**Thread.** This is your choice. Cotton, wool – white or coloured. These are difficult to keep clean, and I prefer nylon single-strand cord ¼ mm in circumference. Drums of this can be purchased in shops dealing with window display supplies (e.g. Dann and Co, 44 Newman Street, London W1. – Cost about £2 for 2,000 m (2384 yds).

**Copper or steel wire.** Purchased from ex-Army stores and junk shops. Buy old flex where the rubber is rotten, and comes off easily. Check that it is perfectly clean, and always lacquer it immediately you strip off the outer covering in order to prevent discoloration. P 61 gives details for using wire in filography.

**Paint.** The board is painted after the nails have been placed in position. A matt black spray gives the best results and shows cotton, metal and nylon to advantage. If you use a brush, matt blackboard paint is used, but be careful not to let the paint clog between the nails. You can choose any colour you like, but always keep a good contrast between the board colour and the thread or wire. A spray paint leaves a pleasant, smooth finish, which is difficult to obtain using a brush. An undercoat may also be necessary.

# Method of construction

**Preparing the board.** First, choose the design that appeals and then draw it carefully to scale on a sheet of paper which is large enough to wrap round the sides of your board. The grid squares in my diagrams will help you to reproduce accurately the lines and angles of the design as you enlarge it. I have in each case suggested a suitable scale for the enlargement of the design, and the number of nails I have specified in each line is correct for this size.

You can, of course, vary the size if you wish, depending on your board (remember that it is desirable to leave a margin of a few centimetres around the design). But if you do not use my suggested scale, you may need more or fewer nails to the line: the closer the nails, the better the result, but it is not practical to have them closer than 2.5 mm (1/10 in). So you will need to work out your optimum number of nails by taking the shortest line and seeing how many will comfortably fit into it. For example, if your shortest line is 9 cm, and you want your nails 3 mm apart, you would work it out as follows, in millimetres:

$90 \div 3 = 30 + 1 = 31$

(you add one because, obviously, the number of nails is always one more than the number of spaces between them)

Having established 31 as your number of nails, see how far apart these should be in the larger lines. Suppose you have a line of 18 cm:

$180 \div 30$ (not 31!) $= 6$

So your nails will be 6 mm apart in this line.

Now, using a ruler or protractor, and a sharp pencil, mark on your paper each nail position. Place the drawing on the sandpapered board, wrap the sides around the edges of the board and fix with strips of Sellotape at the back. Using a bradawl or metal spike, punch a hole through the paper into the board for each nail. Remove the drawing and, by placing the ruler alongside each row of holes, check that all are perfectly straight and the same distance apart.

Using long, pointed pliers, guide each nail into each dent and tap with the hammer; remove pliers and hammer to the correct depth. If in doubt, place a metal bar 6 mm ($\frac{1}{4}$ in) thick alongside, so that you can see exactly how much of the nail is protruding. If a nail is not in far enough, a tap will do, but if you have hammered a nail in too far, the best way is to remove it carefully with pliers, placing a small piece of cardboard on the board where the pliers would touch so you do not mark it during the removal. Then, using a longer nail, hammer it into the hole. This is the main reason why you should choose a thicker board than you apparently need. To straighten the nails in a row, lightly tap with a hammer, and to straighten a nail that is leaning at an angle towards the next one, place the blade of a screwdriver between them, and straighten with a light tap on the end of the screwdriver shaft.

When all the nails are in position, spray with paint. With transparent nylon thread I always choose matt black, but you may prefer some other contrast: a dark purple can give a most interesting effect. Remember that once you start weaving you will not be able to touch up the paint, so spray at least two coats, and check that the edges are not missed – paint is rapidly absorbed and you might find you have to paint the edge with a brush. Be careful not to use too much paint, as a surplus easily clogs at the base of the nails. This is almost bound to occur if you use a brush, nor will you achieve that lovely silky finish that is obtained with a spray; so this is one time when it is worth spending a little more and using the spray. If the wood is porous, spray on an undercoat primer first.

**Weaving.** When the board is completely dry, you are ready to weave the design, using copper or steel flex wire or single nylon thread. (Coloured wool or white cotton give pleasant results, but in damp weather they are inclined to sag and may slip off the nails.) If using wire, please read the section on constructing these projects in schools (*see* p 60), as I have described the procedure there.

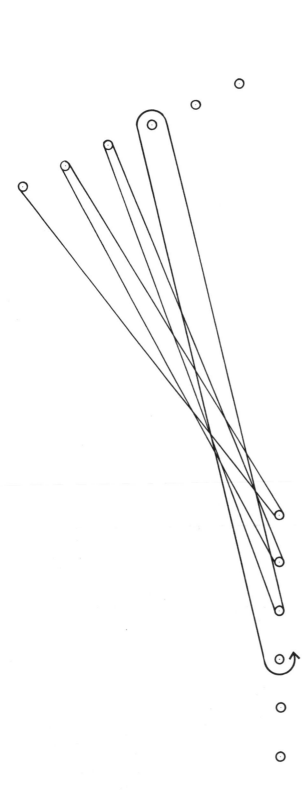
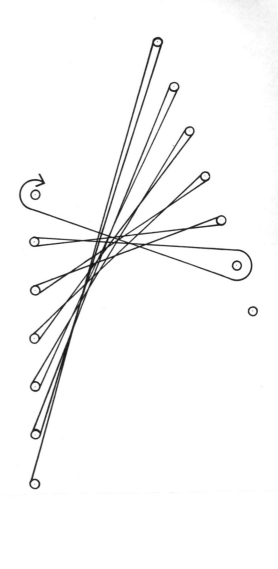

**Method of weaving**

Using nylon thread, start and finish with a reef knot. Keep the thread taut all the time, as even nylon threads expand under damp conditions. This tautness is particularly important when the threads stretch over 30 cm (12 in) between the nails, as in the aircraft wings (*see* p 18), and in this case I suggest the thread be twisted twice round each nail to make it doubly secure (*see* diagram).

In the great majority of my diagrams, rows of nails will be represented by lines, each marked by a letter of the alphabet. The position of the first and last nails will be marked by the relevant figures (1 and 41 in a line consisting of 41 nails, as on p 12); the others can then be inserted at equidistant intervals, once you have worked out their position as described on p8. Thus each nail can be identified by a combination of letter and number, e.g. B2, C13, H6, etc.

The weaving instructions outline in detail the first few moves of any sequence (e.g. for p 12, C41 – B1 – A41 – A40 – B2 – C40 – C39 – B3 – A39) until the pattern of the sequence is clear. It is then easy to continue the pattern in a sequential manner until the final point is reached as stated in the instructions. It is important to take the thread round each nail in the same direction.

**Framing.** Normally I would say 'don't'. The designs should be interesting enough without adding further decoration. But if you prefer a frame, I suggest a copper mount when using copper wire, and chrome or steel when using nylon or steel wire.

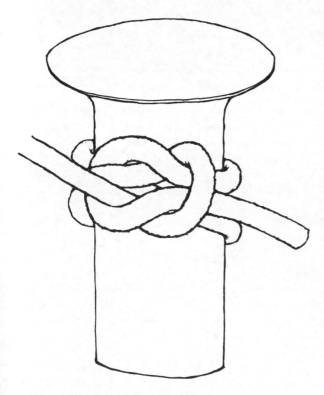

This is a simple knot, firstly tied left over right and secondly right over left.

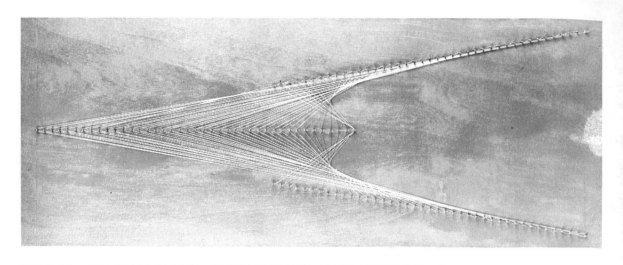

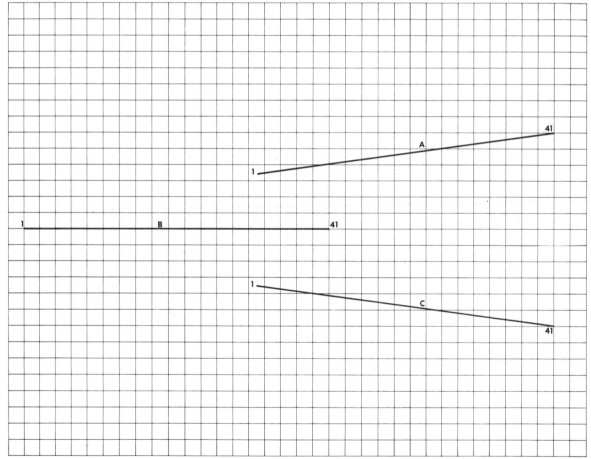

# Elementary designs

These two pages show a couple of easy designs to help you with filography art forms.

A very striking design which shows that the simple shape can often be just as effective as the more complicated ones.

Scale: 1 square = 2.5 cm (1 in)

**Weaving instructions**

C41 – B1 – A41 – A40 – B2 – C40 –
C39 – B3 – A39 – A38 – B4 – C38, etc, to C1.

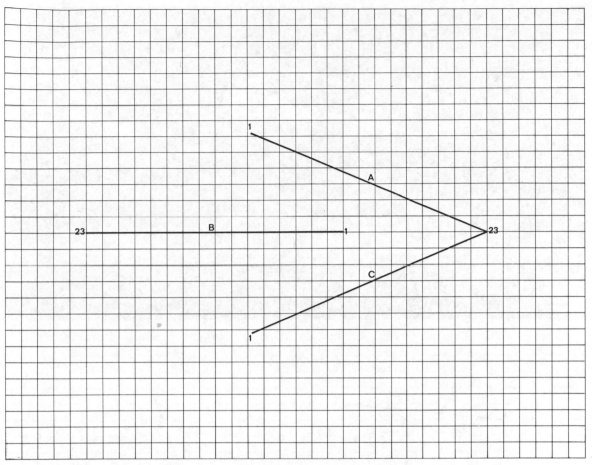

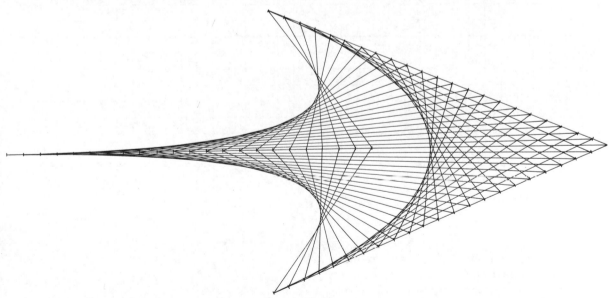

Scale: 4 squares = 2.5 cm (1 in)

**Weaving instructions**

C1 – B1 – A1 – A2 – B2 – C2 – C3, etc, to C23.

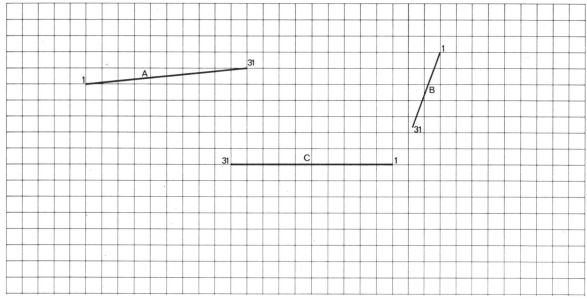

This abstract design should be drawn carefully
on paper first, and by changing the angles and
lengths of the lines, new designs can be evolved.

Scale: 1 square = 2.5 cm (1 in)

**Weaving instructions**
B1 – A1 – C1 –
B2 – A2 – C2, etc, to C31.

## Leather symbol

This is the symbol used to distinguish leather goods. A single thread was used for the weaving.

Scale: 1 square = 1.25 cm (½ in)

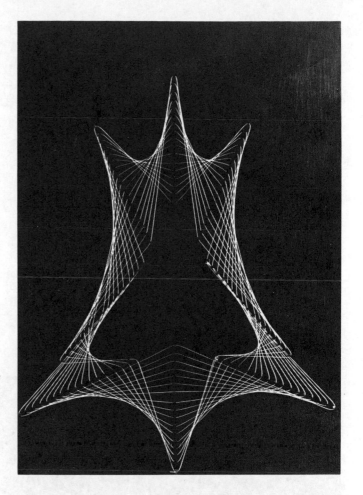

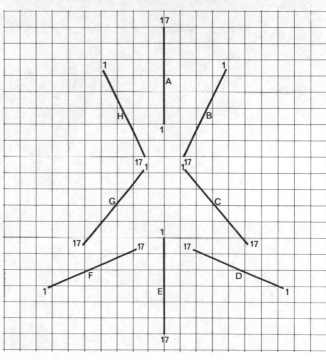

## Weaving instructions

A1 – B1 – C1 – D1 – E1 – F1 – G1 – H1 – A2, etc, to A17.

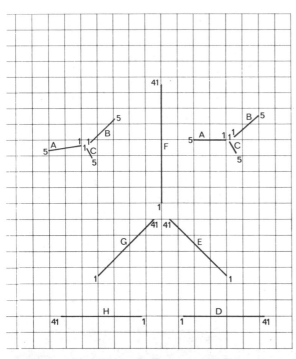

The Eiffel Tower, perhaps?
Scale: 1 square = 2.5 cm (1in)

**Weaving instructions** (*see* note on p 18)

For Seagulls
A5 – C1 – B5 – C1 – A4 – C2 – B4 – C2, etc, to B1.

For Tower
D1 – E1 – F1 – G1 – H1 – H2 – G2 – F2 – E2 –
D2 – D3, etc, to H41.

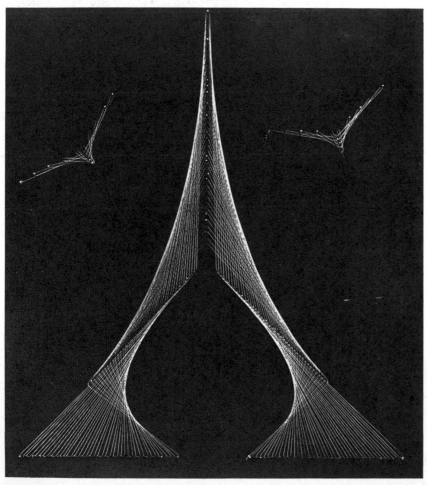

16

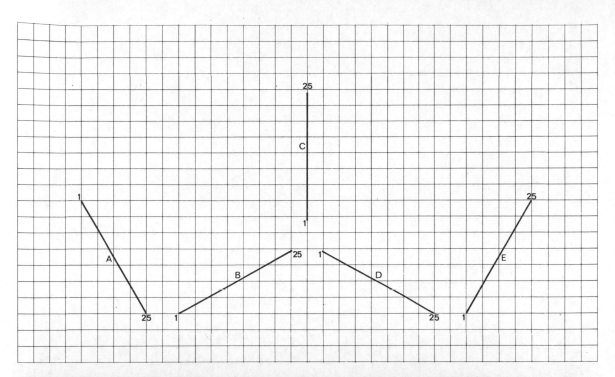

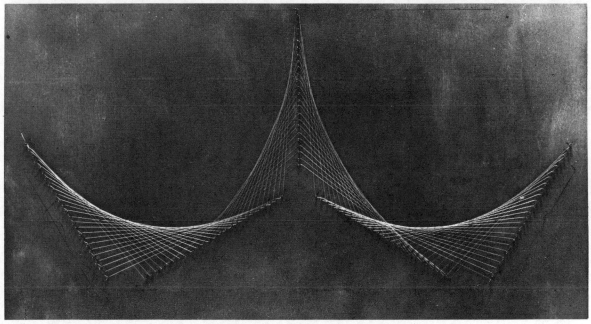

A simple design for you to practise. Later, you could combine it with a circle, as on p 29.

Scale: 1 square = 2.5 cm (1 in)

**Weaving instructions** (*see* note on p 18)
E1 – D1 – C25 – B25 – A25 – A24 – B24 – C24 – D2 –
E2 – E3 – D3 – C23 – B23 – A23 – A22 – B22 –C22 –
D4 – E4, etc, to A1.

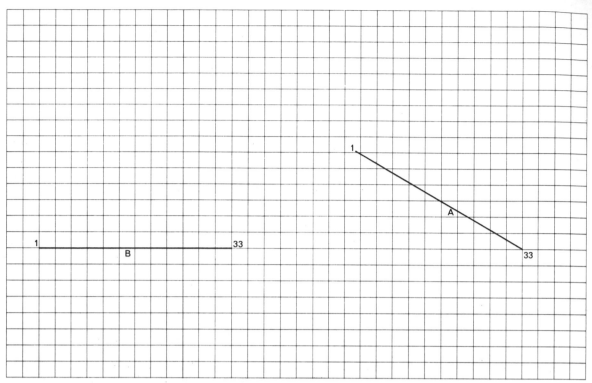

# Aircraft

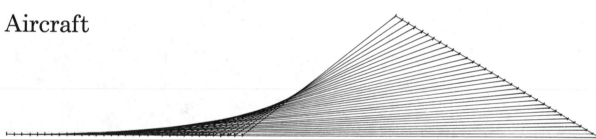

Scale: 1 square = 2.5 cm (1in)

**Weaving instructions**

A1 – B33 – B32 – A2 –
A3 – B31 – B30 – A4, etc, to A33.

The diagrams above show the weaving instructions for an aeroplane wing, and the finished result. You will see how this design is incorporated into the other aircraft designs.

**Note**

These instructions raise a point of technique. When moving from one nail to an adjacent nail in the same row (e.g. A1 – A2), you should execute an 'S' shape with the thread, bringing it round to the *front* of the second nail as shown right. This ensures that the thread lies on the same side of each nail, so that the distance between the threads is constant all the way along the row.

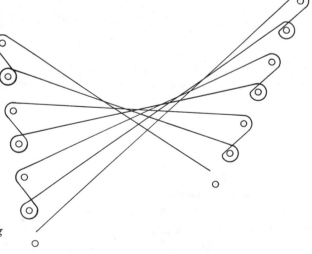

18

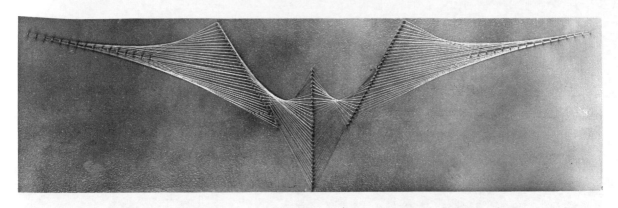

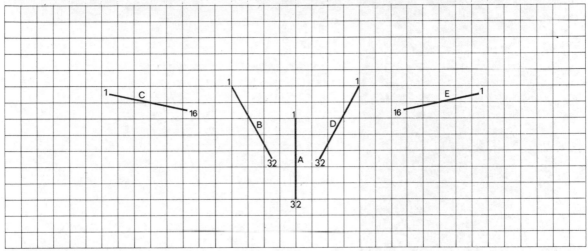

## Concorde

Scale: 1 square = 2.5 cm (1 in)

### Weaving instructions

A1 – B32 – C32 – B1 – A32 – D1 – E32 – D32 – A1 –
A2 – B31 – C31 – B2 – A31 – D2 – E31 – D31 –
A2, etc, to . . . A32 – B1 – C1 – B32 – A1 – D32 –
E1 – D1 – A32.

Another aircraft. Sections of these designs should be included when designing your own styles.

Scale: 1 square = 2.5 cm (1 in)

## Weaving instructions

F26 – C25 – G25 – F25 – C24 – G24, etc, to F1.
D26 – B25 – E25 – D25 – B24 – E24, etc, to D1.
C1 – A25 – B1 – B2 – A24 – C2 – C3 – A23 – B3, etc, to B25.

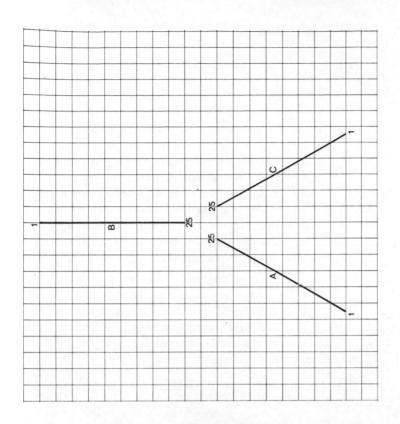

Scale: 4 squares = 2.5 cm (1 in)

**Weaving instructions**

A1 – B25 – C1 – A25 – B1 – C25 –
A2 – B24 – C2 – A24 – B2 – C24, etc, to C1.

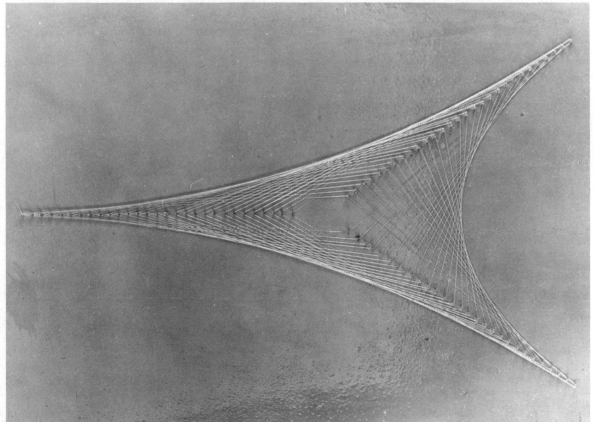

# Circles

First prepare your template. Use a sheet of plain paper the size of the board and on this draw your circle in pencil. Mark a dot at the exact centre of the circle, place a circular plastic protractor on this, and make a small mark on the edge against each ten-degree division. This gives you the thirty-six points.

Now, using a ruler, carefully extend these thirty-six marks to cut the edge of the circle, thus giving the actual nail positions.

Sellotape the paper onto the board, and pierce each nail position with a bradawl. Most designs call for 5 cm (2 in) nails, of which 1.25 cm ($\frac{1}{2}$ in) is hammered into the board.

After painting comes the threading operation. If, however, you decide to glue a sheet of copper over the board to act as the background, this should be glued with Araldite, following the instructions, naturally making sure the board is the correct size first. The template is Sellotaped over this, and the nail positions marked with a bradawl, as before. This procedure is also followed if using a Formica-faced board, as in my sailing ship example (*see* p 48). Very carefully hand-drill each nail hole after removing the paper. If using an electric drill, make sure you pierce only the metal, as a deeper hole will result in loose nails. Be very careful not to scratch the metal surface and protect it when using the hammer, as a bad shot will result in an unsightly dent. The metal should, of course, have been lacquered in the first place to prevent future discoloration.

Using wire or nylon thread, choose any nail and secure the thread with a reef knot. In the diagram count eleven nails, lay your thread around the outside of the nail, pull taut, count to the next eleventh nail, and repeat until every nail in the circle has been used once. If you arrive at a nail that has already been used, stretch the thread outside the edge of the circle to the next unused nail, and continue.

It is important that every thread in the pattern is the same length and at the same angle, or the final pattern will be ruined. When all thirty-six nails have been used, you should find that the thread has arrived back at the nail from which you started. Repeat the process exactly,

constructing a second layer over the first. Then repeat again until you have six similar layers. Keep pressing the thread to the base of each nail.

Now weave another six layers, but counting to every ninth nail. Then weave another six layers using every seventh nail, fifth and, finally, every third nail. If you notice that the thickness of each six layers is taking more or less than a sixth of the height of the nails, you should vary the number of layers, as the aim is to have the nails completely full when the design is complete. Tie a neat reef knot to finish.

Using a new length of thread, tie it to any nail, and run it round and round the outside of the circle, rather like the outside of a drum, until you have filled in the height of the nails. This is a neat finish to the design, and hides all the knots.

The weaving in this example is 3.75 cm (1$\frac{1}{2}$ in) deep. Naturally, if you use 15 or 20 cm (6 to 8 in) nails a very interesting cone shape can be achieved. A further suggestion would be to use dark-coloured threads at the base of the cone, and gradually lighten the shade as the work proceeds. You could also add to the effect by gluing a circular mirror inside the circle of nails at the start.

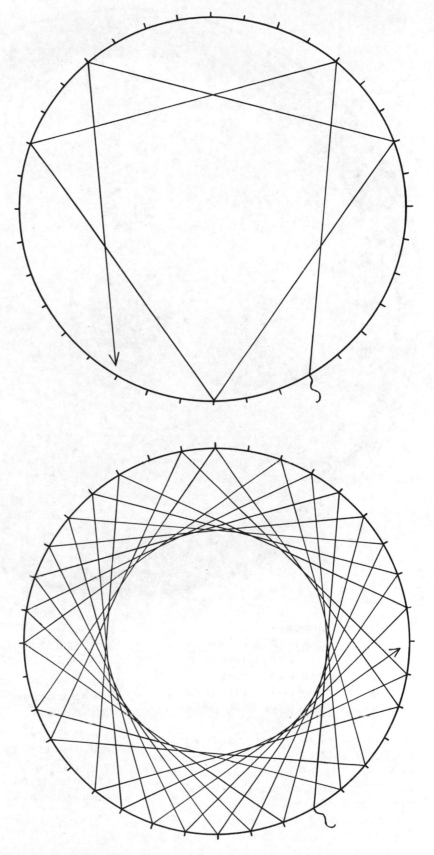

## Weaving instructions

First layer, using every 15th nail: start at 1, then 16 – 31 – 10 – 25, etc, until you have used every nail. Repeat five times more.

Seventh layer, using every 13th nail: start at 3, then 16 – 29 – 6 – 19, etc, as before. Repeat five times more.

Thirteenth layer, using every 11th nail: start at 3, then 14 – 25 – 36, etc. Repeat four times more.

Eighteenth layer, using every 9th nail: start at 3, then 12 – 21 – 30, etc. Repeat three times more.

Twenty-second layer, using every 7th nail: start at 12, then 19 – 26 – 33, etc. Repeat twice more.

Twenty-fifth layer, using every 5th nail: start at 12, then 17 – 22 – 27, etc. Finish.

Now wind your thread or wire round and round the outer drum of nails until only the tips are left showing.

This is woven on a copper plate, on the back of which has been glued a circle of wood about 2.5 cm (1 in) thick the same size. The holes are drilled in the copper plate and the nails are hit through these holes into the wood.

24

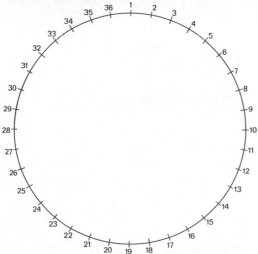

### Another circle

You can obviously make your own versions by varying the number of layers and by counting off different numbers of nails with your thread; you should start with a higher number (as long as it is less than half the total number of nails) and continue with successively smaller numbers (every 15th, every 13th, etc). Or you can have twice the number of nails, as above.

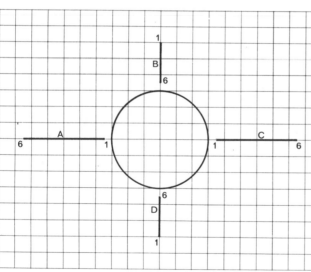

When you have mastered the circle,
it can be incorporated into many designs.
This one is done on teak with steel wire.

Scale: 1 square = 2.5 cm (1 in)

**Weaving instructions**
A1 – B1 – C1 – D1 – A1 –
A2 – B2 – C2 – D2 – A2, etc, to . . .
A6 – B6 – C6 – D6 – A6.
Circle: *see* p 22/3

Scale:
1 square = 19 mm (¾ in)

**Weaving instructions**

For the two longer points:
B1 – A16 – A1 – B15 – A2,
etc, to B2 – A15 – B1.
For the shorter ones:
B1 – A10 – A1 – B9 – A2,
etc, to B2 – A9 – A1.

Circles: each circle has
36 nails; *see* p 22-3 for
construction.

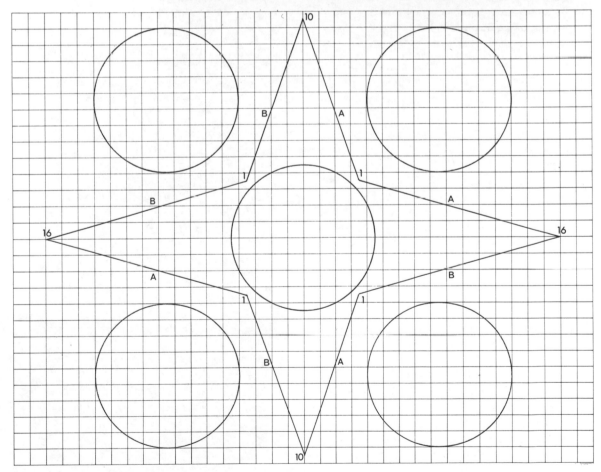

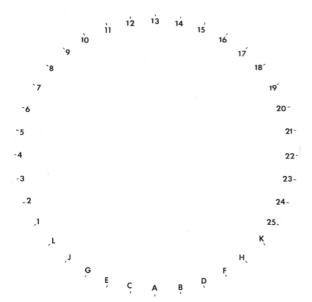

## Circles (pineapple shape)

Here is another way to weave a circle (or a cone).
Choose a number of your nails – always an odd
number – as 'base' nails (here lettered A – L).
Weaving instructions are given below, and
the diagrams show stages in the building up of
the design, using 36 nails.

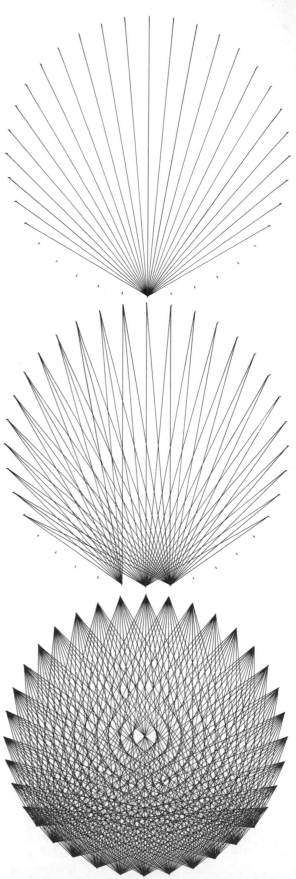

## Weaving instructions

A – 1 – A – 2 – A – 3 – A – 4 – A, etc, to 25 – A
Finish with a reef knot.
With new thread, B – 1 – B – 2 – B – 3 – B – 4 – B,
etc, to 25 – B. Similarly, C – 1 – C – 2 – C, etc, to
25 – C (*see* diagram).
Continue with D, E, F, etc (note how your base
nail will be alternately on the left and the right),
until you have completed L.

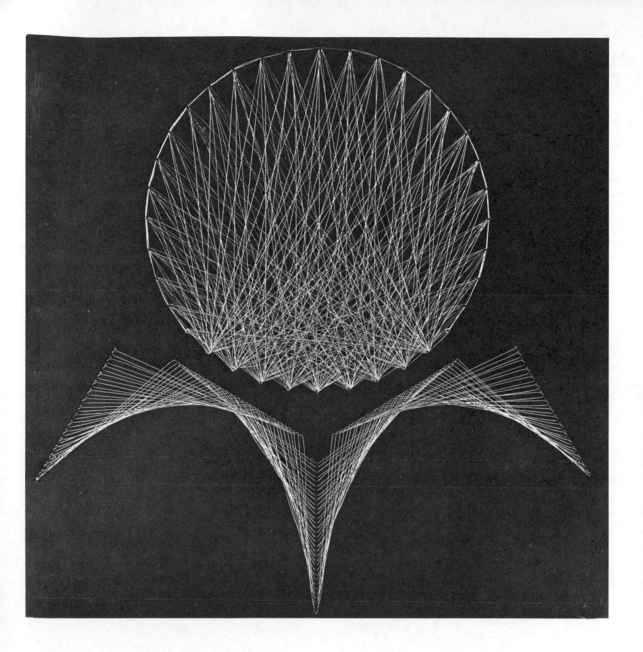

This design incorporates the pineapple-shaped
circle and an abstract similar to that on p 17.
The circle has 36 nails but differs from the one
on page 28 in that only 9 base nails have been
worked. Weaving instructions would therefore
be A – 1 – A – 2 – A – 3, etc, to 27; and then with a
new thread B – 1 – B – 2 – B – 3, etc, to 27 until the
circle is finished. Complete the circle by
threading round the outside of the nails.

The base is made up of 5 lines of 33 nails each and
the same weaving instructions as on p 17 apply,
but obviously with adjustment for the extra nails
used here.

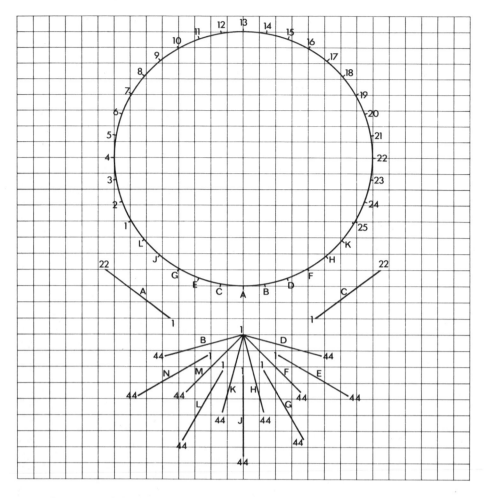

A combination of the 'pineapple' circle with the
design on p 37. Without doubt, this is my
favourite design. The circle needs strong nails.

Scale: 1 square = 2.5 cm (1 in)

**Weaving instructions**

*Base design*

B1 – A1 – B44 – B43 – A2 – B2 –
B3 – A3 – B42 – B41 – A4 – B4, etc, to
B21 – A21 – B24 – B23 – A22 – B22.

D1 – C1 – D44 – D43 – C2 – D2 –
D3 – C3 – D42 – D41 – C4 – D4, etc, to
D21 – C21 – D24 – D23 – C22 – D22.

B44 – N1 – M44 – L1 – K44 – J1 – H44 – G1 – F44 –
E1 – D44 – D43 – E2 – F43 – G2 – H43 – J2 – K43
– L2 – M43 – N2 – B43, etc, to D1.

*Circle: see p 28/9.*

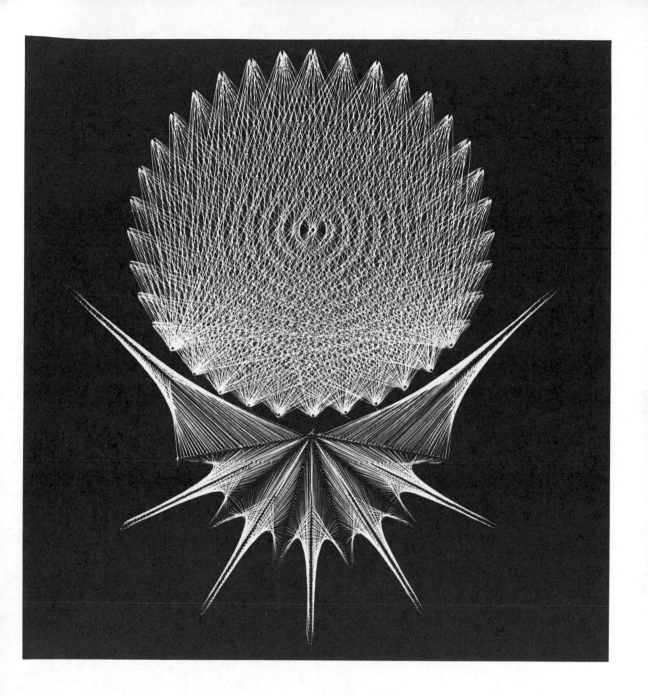

### Pineapple with base leaves

The plate in the colour section shows how the 'pineapple' design can be used for a cone shape, so that the result really is a pineapple! Weaving instructions are the same as on p 28-9, with eleven 'base' nails. The weaving grid for the base leaves can be made up from the colour plate.

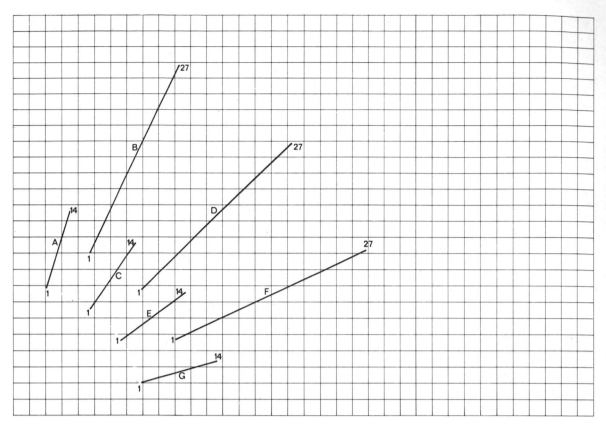

# Stars

The diagram shows a section of a star, and can be used as a practice project before you attempt the complete stars on the following pages.
Scale: 1 square = 1.25 cm ($\frac{1}{2}$ in)

**Weaving instructions**
A1 – B27 – C1 – D27 – E1 – F27 – G1 – F25 – E1 –
D25 – C1 – B25 – A1 – A2 – B23 – C2 – D23 – E2 –
F23 – G2 – F21 – E2 – D21 – C2 – B21 – A2 – A3,
etc, to C14 – B1 – A14.

G14 – E1 – C14 – A1 – A2 – C13 – E2 –
G13 – G12 etc, to G1.

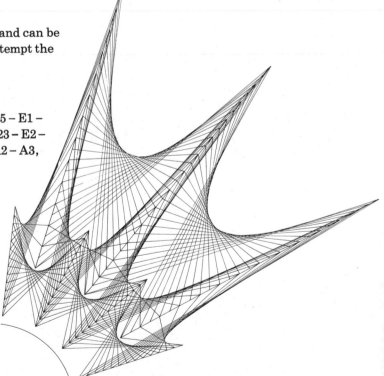

1 Pineapple with base leaves (p30)

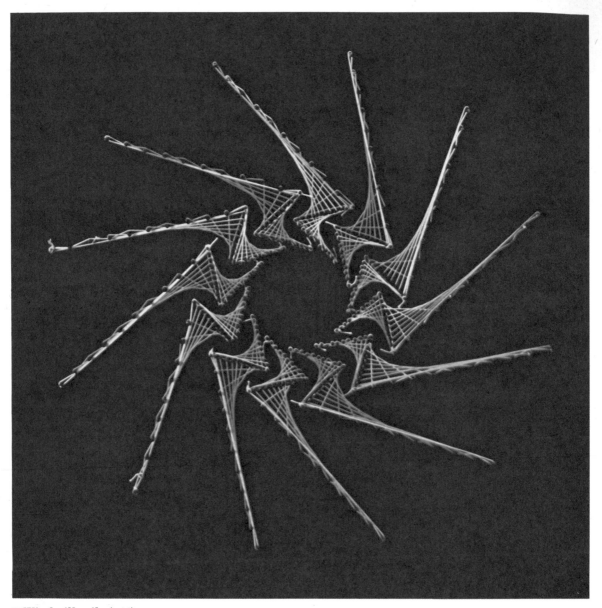

2 Windmill sails (p44)

**3** Maltese cross woven on a matt black background (p50)

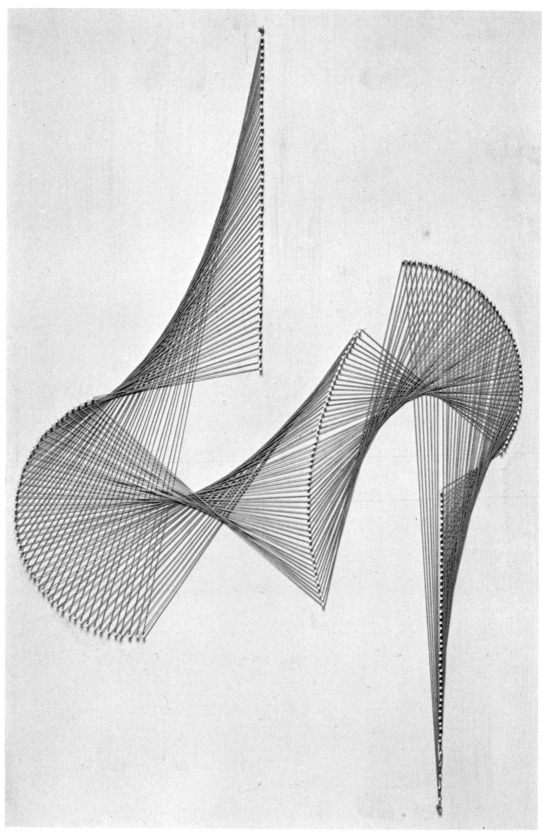

4 Abstract design woven in blue cotton (p42)

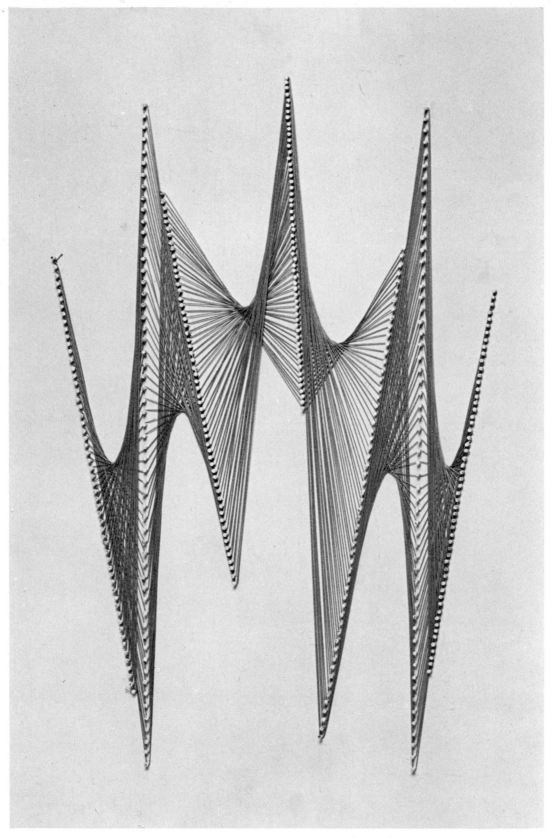

5 Elizabeth of Hungary's crown (p54)

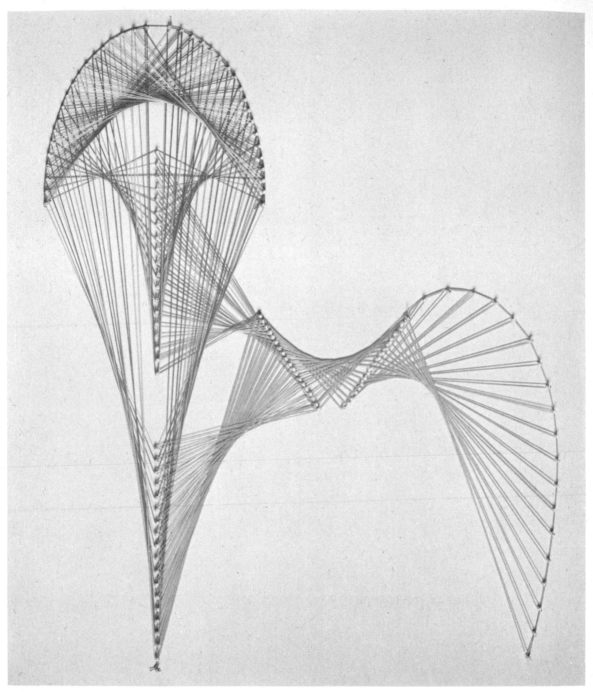

**6** Single-winged eagle (p46)　　　　　　　　　**7** Sailing ship (p48)

**8** Vintage car (p60)

**9** Womble (p61)

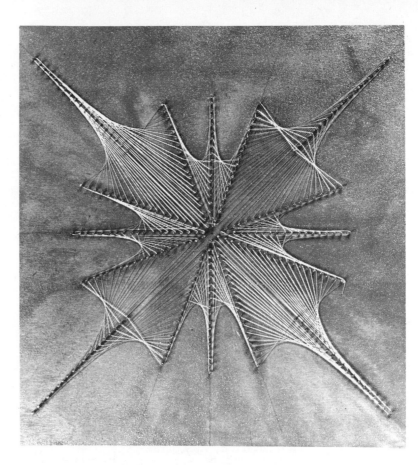

This star, or variations, is used in many designs.
Scale: 1 square = 1.25 cm
($\frac{1}{2}$ in)

**Weaving instructions**
A19 – B1 – C1 – D1 – E19 – F1 –
G1 – H1 – J19 – K1, etc, to
Q1 – A18 – B2 – C2 – D2 – E18 –
F2 – G2 – H2 – J18 – K2, etc, to
Q2 – A17, etc.
Continue thus to A1 – B19 –
C19 – D19 – E1 – F19 – G19 –
H19 – J1 – K19, etc, to Q19.
Note that when a number of
nails come close together in
the centre of a circle, you can
either space them out slightly
as in this illustration or use
one nail twice to represent the
end of 2 lines.

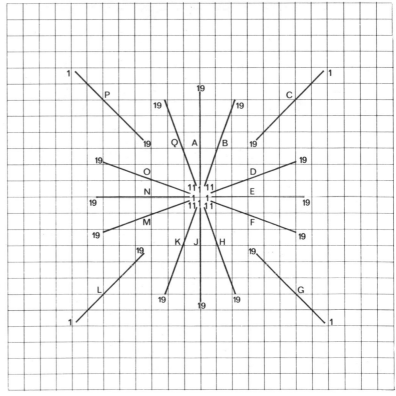

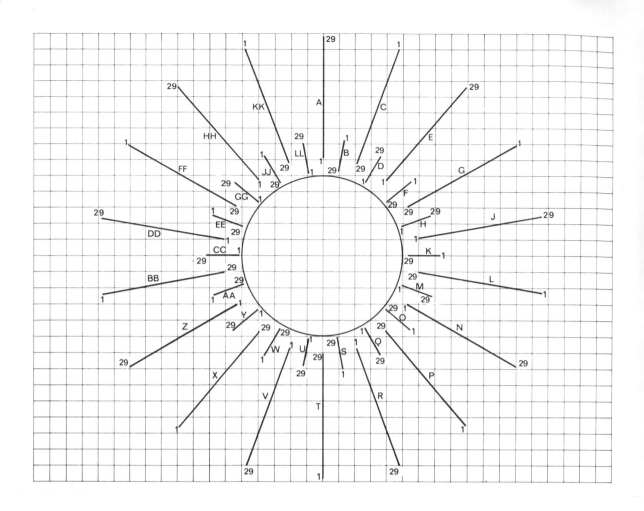

The best of both worlds – 'pineapple' circle and star combined. Although it looks complicated, it is in fact a very easy pattern to weave, if time consuming.

The inner circle consists of 36 nails set just inside the ends of the radiating lines; 11 base nails have been worked. It is better to keep the two figures separate and not to make some nails common to both.

Scale: 1 square = 2.5 cm (1 in)

**Weaving instructions**

A1 – C1 – E1 – G1 – J1 – L1, etc, to KK1 – A2 – C2, etc, to KK29 – A29.

A1 – B1 – C29 – D29 – E1 – F1, etc, to LL29 – A2 – B2, etc, to LL1 – A29.

B29 – D29 – F29 – H29 – K29, etc, to LL29 – B28 – D28, etc, to LL1 – B1.

Circle: *see* p 28/9.

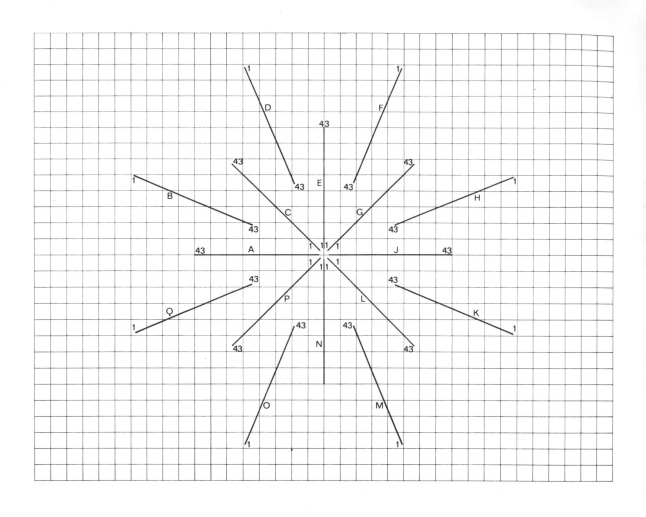

Scale: 1 square = 2.5 cm (1 in)

**Weaving instructions**

A1 – B1 – C1 – D1 – E1 – F1 – G1 – H1 – J1 – K1 –
L1 – M1 – N1 – O1 – P1 – Q1 – A2, etc, to Q43 – A43.
A1 – C43 – E1 – G43 – J1 – L43 – N1 – P43 – A2, etc,
to P1 – A43.

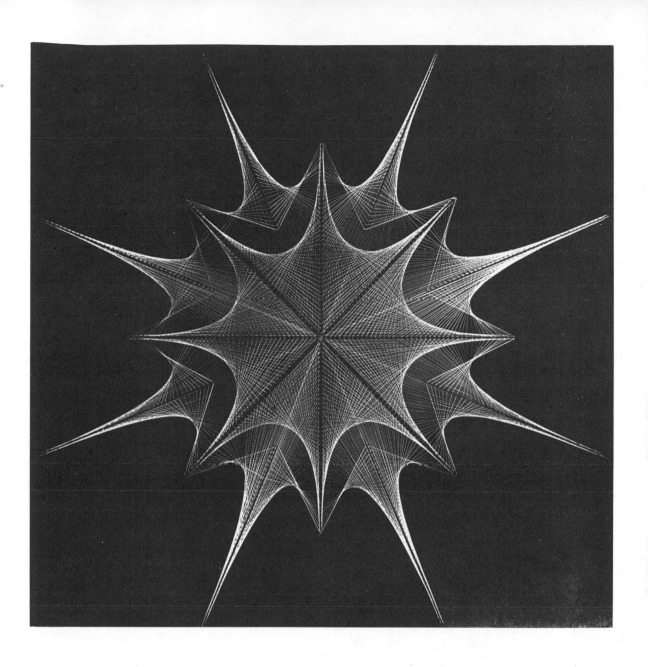

# Abstracts

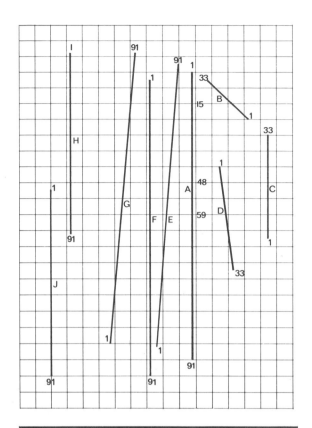

Scale: 1 square = 2.5 cm (1 in)

**Weaving instructions**

A1 – E1 – F1 – G1 – H1 – H2 – G2 – F2 – E2 – A2, etc, to A91.

G1 – J1 – G2 – J2, etc, to J91.

D1 – A91 – B33 – A48 – D2 – A90 – B32 – A47 - D3, etc, to D33 – A59 – B1 – A1.

B1 – C1 – D1 – B2, etc, to D33.

Opposite:

Scale: 1 square = 2.5 cm (1 in)

**Weaving instructions**

A1 – B1 – C1 – A2 – B2 – C2, etc, to C52.

D1 – E1 – F1 – D2 – E2 – F2, etc, to F52.

G1 – B52 – H1 – J1 – K1 – E52 – G71 – G70 – E51 – K2 – J2 – H2 – B51 – G2 – G3, etc, to G52. You can see in the photograph how this results in an overlapping of strands along part of row G.

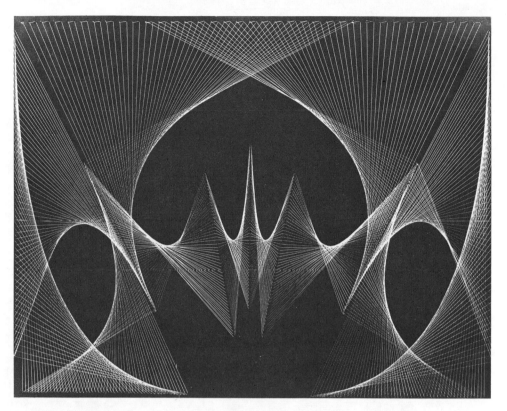

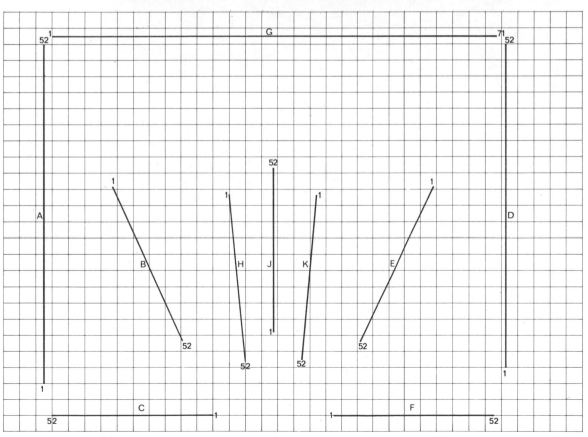

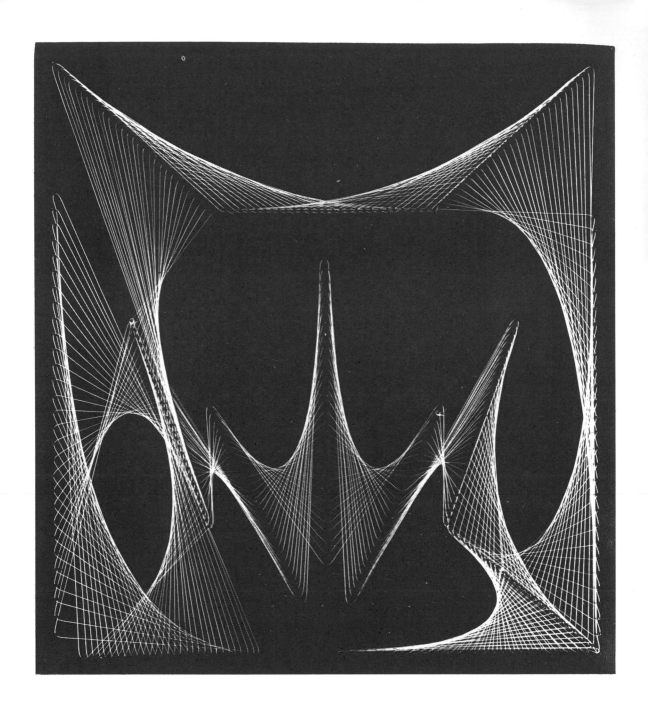

Another abstract, but this one is not entirely
symmetrical.

Scale: 1 square = 1.25 cm (½ in)

**Weaving instructions**

A1 – B1 – C1 – D1 – E1 – F29 – G1 – H29 – J1 – K29
– A2, etc, to K1 – A29.

F29 – N1 – F28 – N2 – F27 – N3, etc, to N29.

M1 – A29 – L1 – M2 – A28 – L2 – M3, etc, to L29.

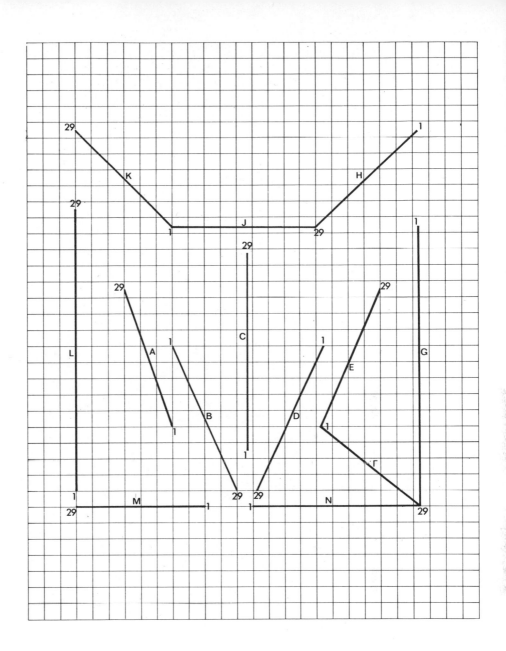

Scale: 1 square = 1.25 cm (½ in)

**Weaving instructions**

A1 – B49 – C1 – D1 – E49 – E48 – D2 – C2 – B48, etc, to E1.

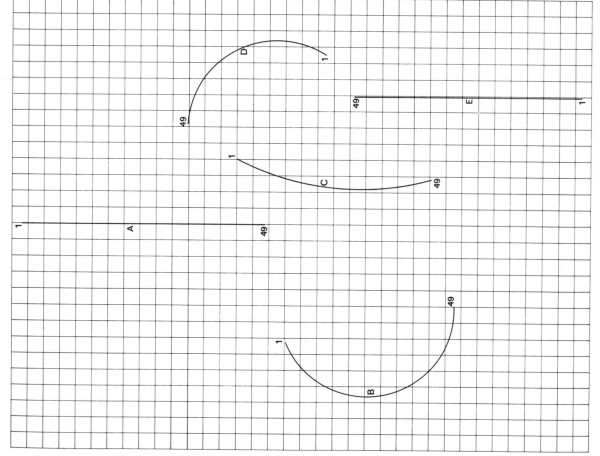

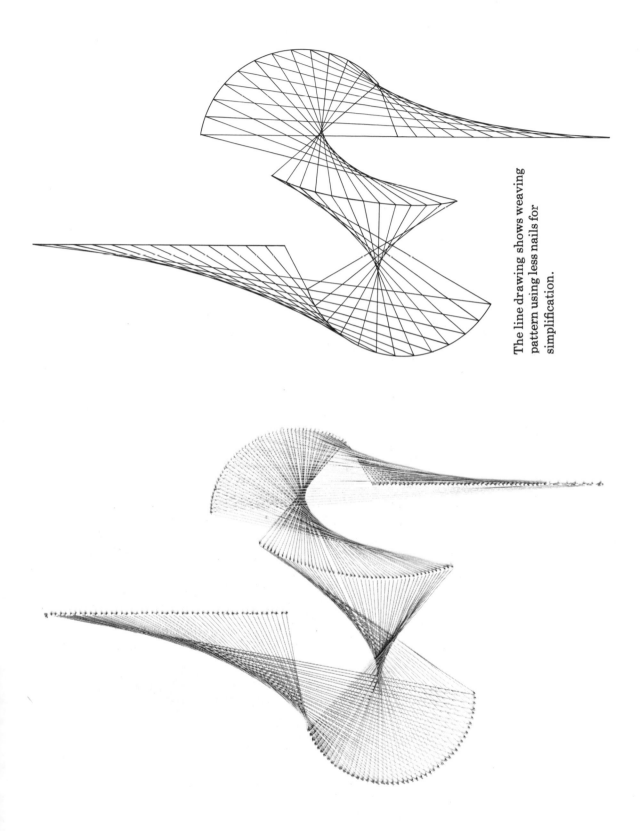

The line drawing shows weaving pattern using less nails for simplification.

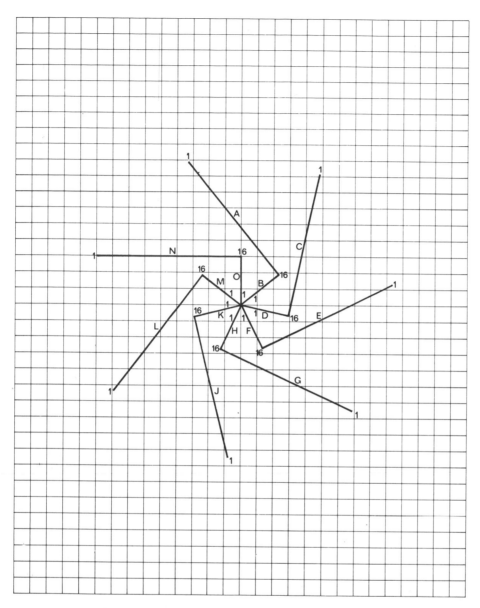

# Windmill sails

Scale: 1 square $= 1.25\,\text{cm}\ (\tfrac{1}{2}\,\text{in})$
Centre angles: $\frac{360}{7} = 51\,\tfrac{3}{7}$ degrees

**Weaving instructions**
B1 – A16 – B2 – A15 – B3 – A14, etc, to A1, then
A16 – D1 – C16 – D2 – C15 – D3, etc, to C1 – C16 –
F1, etc. Continue thus for each sail.

The result will be neater if one nail only is used
in the centre – to do duty for B1, D1, F1, H1, K1,
M1 and O1.

44

*See* colour plate for another windmill. The grid
can be made up from the illustration, and the
centre angles are $\frac{360}{12} = 60$ degrees.

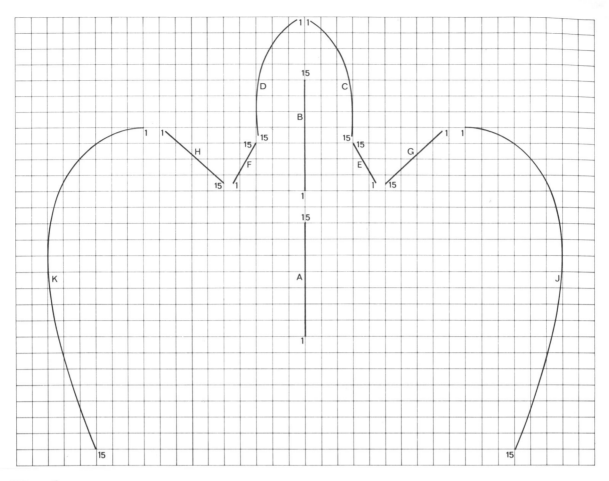

# Eagle

**Single-winged eagle** *see* colour plate and
cover which show part of this design done with 19
nails instead of 15 in each row. Weaving
instructions are exactly the same, allowing for
the extra nails.

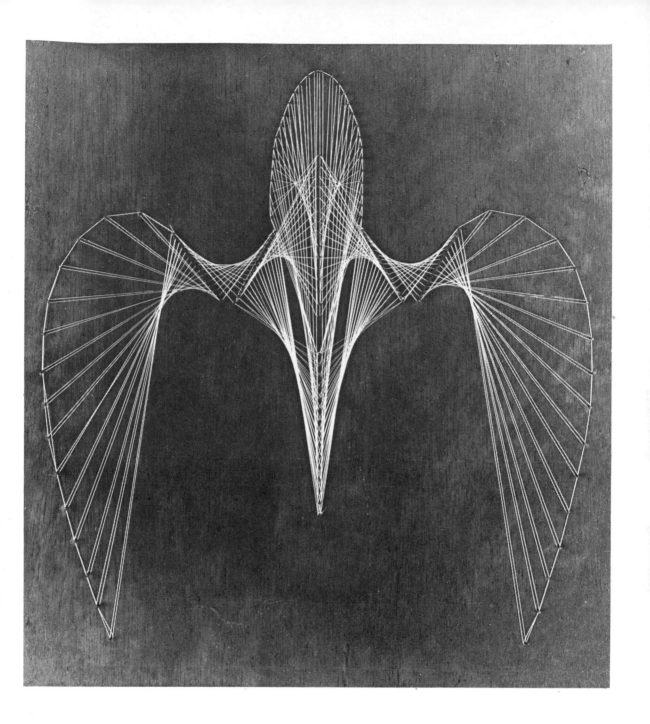

## Double-winged eagle

Scale: 1 square·= 2.5 cm (1 in)

**Weaving instructions**

A1 – C1 – B1 – D1 – A2 – C2 – B2 – D2, etc, to D15.

A15 – E1 – G1 – J15 – G1 – E1 –
A14 – E2 – G2 – J14 – G2 – E2, etc, to E15 – A1.

A15 – F1 – H1 – K15 – H1 – F1 –
A14 – F2 – H2 – K14 – H2 – F2, etc, to F15 – A1.

E1 – B15 – F1 – F2 – B14 – E2 –
E3 – B13 – F3 – F4 – B12 – E4, etc, to F15.

Run thread round the outline of the wings and fasten off at J14 and K14.

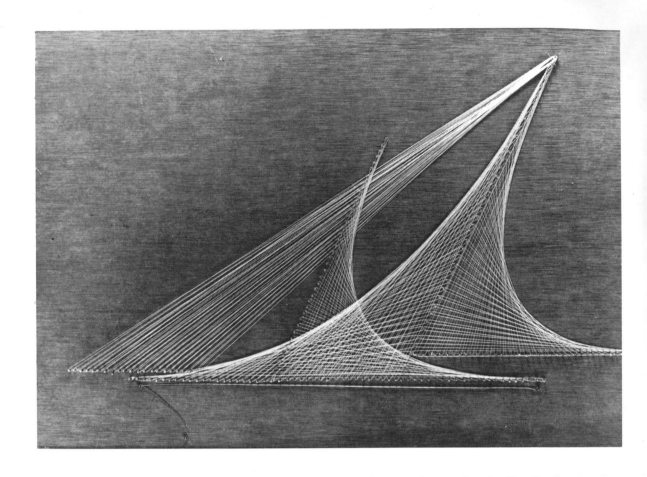

# Sailing ship

(*see* colour plate)

My sailing ship was constructed on a Formica-covered board (*see* p 22 for copper- or Formica-covered boards), and the outline of the hull is a length of copper wire, lacquered (*see* p 61 for instructions concerning copper wire). Great care must be taken to prevent the Formica from splitting when hammering in the nails; I lightly tapped a sharp bradawl into each nail position first.

This is an example where one series of nylon strands overlaps another series of nails, and care must be taken that they are evenly spaced as they pass between the nails. Use a double-size nail at the top of the mast to take the strain of the twenty-odd strands.

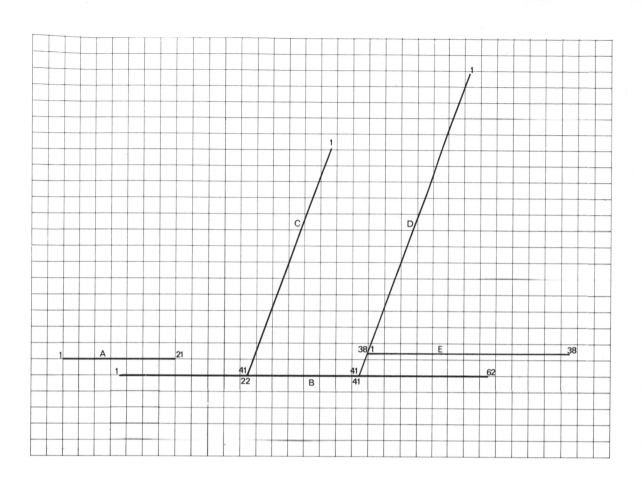

**Weaving instructions for sails**

A1 – D1 – A2 – D1 – A3 – D1, etc, to A21.
B22 – C1 – B23 – C2, etc, to B62 – C41.
E1 – D1 – E2 – D2, etc, to E38 – D38.
B41 – D1 – B40 – D2 – etc, to B1 – D41.

Scale: 1 square = 1.25 cm ($\frac{1}{2}$ in)

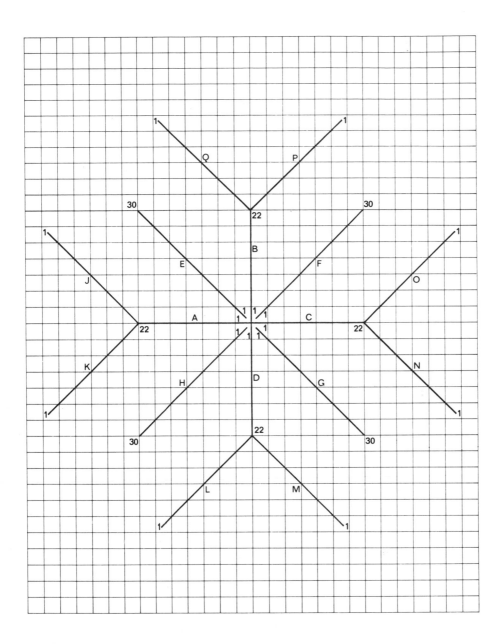

# Maltese cross (*see* colour plate)

Scale: 1 square = 1.25 cm ($\frac{1}{2}$ in)

**Weaving instructions**

K22 – A1 – J22 – K1 – A22 – J1 – K22 – K21 – A2 –
J21 – K2 – A21 – J2 – K21 – K20 – A3, etc, to
K10 – A10 – J10 – K11 – A11 – J11 – K11.
Repeat this for the other three sections,
beginning Q22, O22 and M22. (*See* note on p 33
regarding nail positions in centre of design.)

H1 – E30 – F1 – G30 – H1 – H2 – E29 – F2 – G29 –
H2 – H3 – E28 – F3 – G28 – H3, etc, to
H30 – E1 – G1 – H30.

Tudor rose

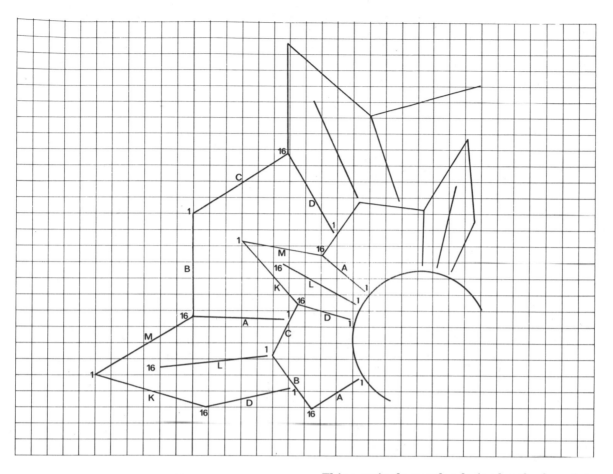

This seemingly complex design breaks down into a 36-nail circle with the two basic shapes shown in the diagram; these two shapes are used five times to surround the circumference of the circle and then, slightly larger, another five times round the outside of the design (*see* diagram for the way in which the larger set fits round the smaller; you should use this figure to construct your own design to scale). The weaving instructions are for the two basic shapes and are simply repeated for each of the ten sections making up the complete figure.

**Weaving instructions**
A1 – B16 – C1 – D16 – D15 – C2 – B15 – A2 – A3, etc, to A16.
K1 – L1 – M1 – M2 – L2 – K2 – K3, etc, to K16.

Circle: 1st layer, every 15th nail.
2nd layer, every 11th nail.
3rd layer, every 7th nail.

The Tudor rose shown here is on a 60 cm (2 ft) square board.

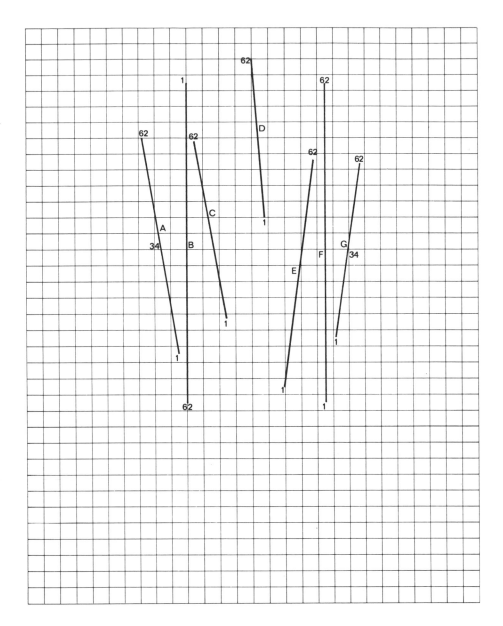

# Elizabeth of Hungary's Crown

This magnificent design was given me by a friend, and I cannot improve on it. I made my version very large, but you can work a smaller one by making one square of the grid equal to, say, 6.5 cm (2½ in), and reducing the number of nails in proportion. Care must be taken where one series of nylon threads crosses the line of nails of another part, to ensure that all the threads are perfectly regular.

Scale: 1 square = 14 cm (5½ in)

**Weaving instructions**

A1 – B1 – C1 – D62 – E1 – F62 – G1 – G2 – F61 – E2, etc, to A62.

C1 – E62 – C2 – E61 – C3, etc, to E1.

C1 – G62 – C2 – G61 – C3, etc, to G1.

A1 – E62 – A2 – E61 – A3, etc, to E1.

A1 – G34 – A2 – G33 – A3 – G32, etc, to A34 – G1.

Note that in the colour plate, only the first section of the instructions has been worked; the last four sections have been omitted.

# Catherine wheel

This is the most difficult design I have ever attempted. As you can see from the photograph, the nails are arranged in a series of diminishing spirals, the nails themselves becoming steadily closer together as they approach the middle of the spiral. So, instead of a scale drawing, I have given a diagram of the actual nail positions for the wheel (*see* p 58/9). If you trace this you will have a complete diagram of the nail positions which you can transfer to your board in the usual way.

I have given each spiral line of nails a letter, from A to M, and there are 50 nails in each row. I have labelled the first and last nails in each line (1 and 50), 1 is always the outermost nail of each line, 50 the innermost.

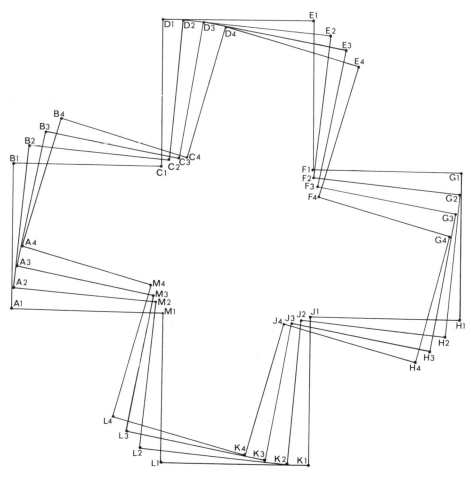

Once your diagram is labelled correctly, the weaving instructions are simple:

A1 – B1 – C1 – D1 – E1 – F1 – G1 – H1 – J1 – K1 – L1 – M1 – A1 – A2 – B2 – C2 – D2, etc, to M2 – A2 – A3, etc, to M50.

You will find that your thread makes a series of 'boxes' which become gradually smaller as you move towards the centre; the diagram shows the appearance of the thread after four rounds of weaving.

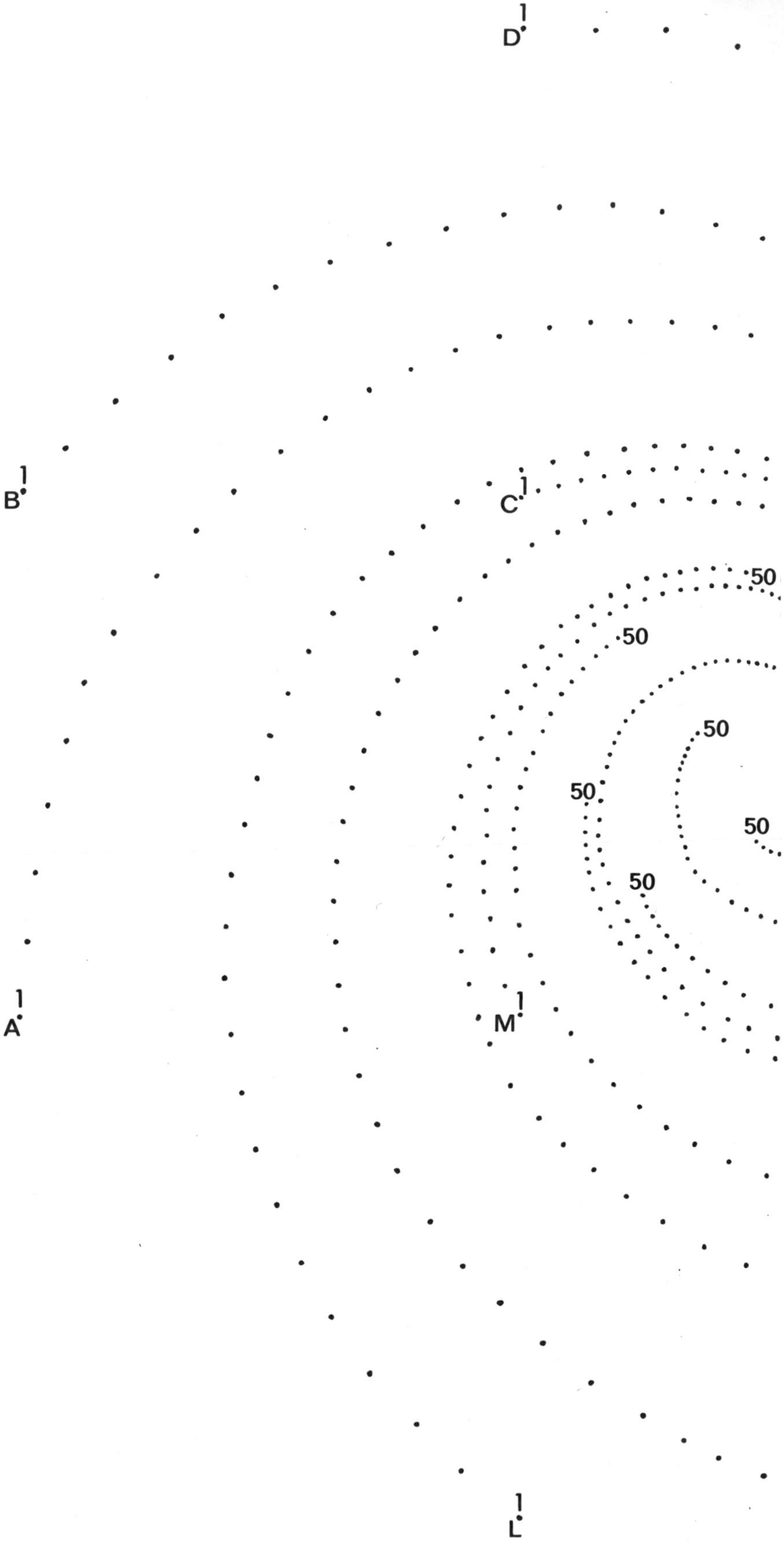
D
1
B
1
C
1
50
50
50
50
50
50
A
1
M
1
L
1

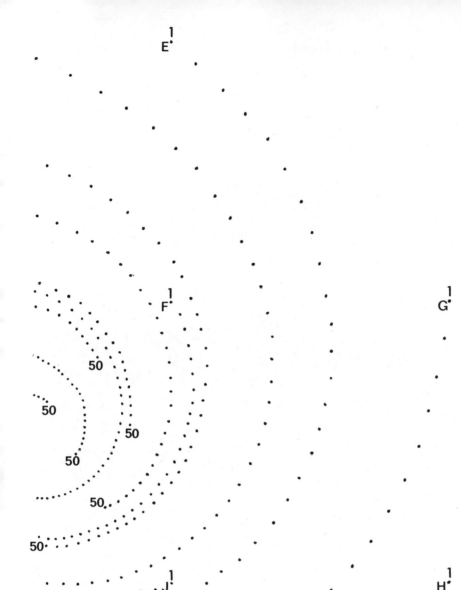

# Filography for children and schools

This is an ideal subject for children of all ages and develops artistic skills, as well as providing a lasting, attractive picture to hang on the wall. Two examples are shown, a vintage car from the London to Brighton race, and a pennyfarthing bicycle. These subjects, besides being simple to construct, are of interest to children – in fact any line drawing can be used which is not too complicated. The basic instructions are the same as those given in the Introduction, but there are some points on which it is worth enlarging.

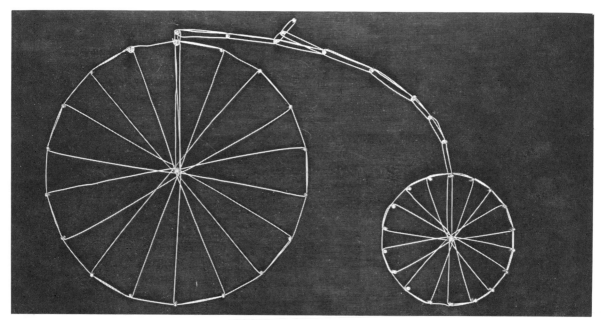

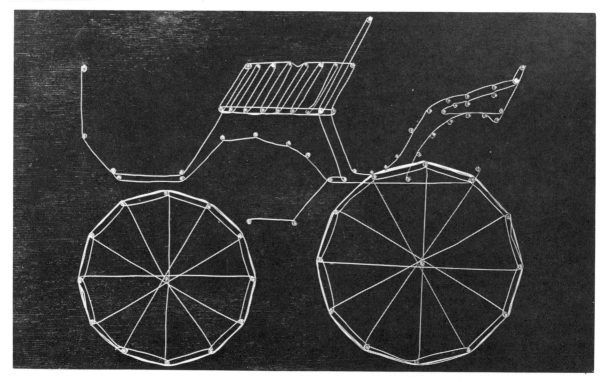

**Materials.** When constructing a design of some object which is made of metal, as in my two examples, choose a metal wire, copper or steel; similarly, nylon thread is more suitable for the sails of a ship. The panel or veneer pins used with nylon thread have hardly any heads at all, but wire is more difficult to keep taut and therefore copper nails with fairly large heads should be used. I buy them by the pound (weight) in any good hardware store. In most examples the painting is carried out after the nails have been hammered into the board, as this helps to make the nails disappear so that only the design is visible. But in the two designs shown, the nails represent rivets and are part of the design, so I painted the board with matt blackboard paint before hammering in the nails.

As both my examples are threaded with wire, I have reserved my instructions for wire until now; instructions for nylon thread have already been given in the Introduction (*see* p 8). Drums of steel wire can be bought at do-it-yourself shops, but make sure that the wire has not become discoloured and lacquer it immediately to prevent this. Fuse wire, you will find, is too expensive to be practicable.

Copper wire can be purchased from any shop specializing in second-hand electrical parts; you simply ask for old electric flex. Make sure that the rubber outer covering is rotten enough to be torn off with your fingers; I can assure you from experience that trying to remove metres of rubber covering with a wire stripper is quite impossible, and if you try to burn off the rubber you will blacken the wire.

At the same time as you strip off the outer covering, it is essential to run the wire through a cloth heavily impregnated with clear lacquer. If this is not done, the wire will corrode, and trying to clean or polish yards of wire is not an enviable job. After laying newspaper over my kitchen pulley, I place the wire on this to dry (be careful not to cause any kinks). When dry, carefully wind the wire onto a drum. If wound before it is dry, the lacquered strands stick to each other and are useless.

The vintage car and pennyfarthing bicycle (opposite) were worked on a board 30 cm by 20 cm (12 in by 8 in).

**Positioning the nails.** A careful and exact drawing of the object should be made on a sheet of paper large enough for the edges to be wrapped round the board and Sellotaped to the back. A small pencil cross is made on the paper for each nail. For the vintage car I used a small protractor over the wheels and drew each spoke at an angle of 30 degrees. The positions of the other nails do not have to be exact: I suggest that on a straight line a nail each end is sufficient; on a gentle curve place a nail every 1.25 cm ($\frac{1}{2}$ in), and on an abrupt curve every 6mm ($\frac{1}{4}$ in). Study the photograph opposite and you will see clearly how this is done.

Using a sharp bradawl, make a hole through the paper into the board for each nail, and then remove the drawing. Instructions for hammering the nails will be found in the Introduction on p 9.

**Threading the wire.** You will require wire snippers to cut the ends of the wire and a pair of pliers to pull it taut as it is used. A piece of cardboard should be fixed in the jaws of the pliers, so that the lacquer is not scratched off the wire.

Unroll a few more centimetres of wire than you need, twist the end three times round the base of the first nail and tighten the twist with pliers. Twist round the next nail and continue. If the wire is not perfectly straight, carefully pull it taut with the pliers. When the last nail of the section is reached, twist the end round three times, tighten with the pliers, snip off the end and start on the next section. You can see now why designs should be kept simple and straight-forward. Too much detail in your original drawing could easily result in a mess.

If you want to hang your picture, you will need three eyescrews and a length of picture wire. Attach the screws to the back of the board, one in each top corner (for the wire) and one farther down, in the middle of the board; this will allow the board to hang straight, instead of tilting against the wall.

# Designing your own filograph

To make your own designs will, I hope, be your aim.

About six designs in this book are not original, and were seen either at Thames Embankment exhibitions, or given to me by friends; as I do not know the originators I can only trust they have no objection to my using them. All the other designs are either variations or original ideas, often worked out in the train to town, or returning from business.

The satisfaction obtained when a 'doodle' gradually forms a constructive design can be likened to that of a rose grower who, after examining ten thousand seedlings, selects a Peace, or a Queen Elizabeth.

A close study of the designs will show how one develops from another; by selecting a small section, slightly changing the angle of one row of nails, lengthening one row, joining it to another section, a new creation is born.

When using nylon thread you will notice that the finished design has very attractive shading effects, especially if you use a spotlight on it; although this is not obvious from the pencil drawing, as you become experienced you will be able to take this effect into consideration when designing.

While complicated designs such as the Tudor Rose have their place, I feel that the simpler the design, the stronger the effect delights the eye. Colour and contrast play their part; quite a stunning result is obtained by pasting black velvet over the board, and then constructing the design with gold thread or lacquered copper wire.

The photograph shows how one sketch can develop into another. The first one is a fish. Using the weaving method of the 'pineapple' (*see* p 28), you can construct a pelican.

*The Womble* (*see* colour plate) is a good example of the scope of filography. Woven in cotton by Michael Scott Baker. With the exception of his fingers he is woven at random using a master pin and working to approximately eight other pins, then another master pin is selected. Take the cotton round the first pin clockwise, the second pin anticlockwise, the third clockwise etc, to give depth. The fingers were woven as follows: 1 nail at the tip of the finger is woven to each of the pins at the base of the finger; this is repeated for each nail at the tip, thus forming the knuckles. The cotton is taken round the master pin clockwise and round the base nail anticlockwise.

# Pan Craft Books

A new series of large-format books, with many full-colour illustrations, for the age of leisure.

Amongst this fast-growing series you will find:

## Macramé 95p

Mary Walker Phillips

Macramé has been defined as the interknotting of yarns. It is, however, much more than that. The real wonder of Macramé is that anything as simple can produce such a variety of beautiful things and create such fun in making them – among the numerous projects the author has designed exclusively for the book are belts, sashes, hanging plant-holders, cushion covers, wall hangings, rugs, necklaces and bracelets.

## Jewellery 95p

Thomas Gentille

Making jewellery is not nearly as difficult as is generally supposed. Its basic processes are few and can be learned quickly, and it is a craft that can be easily practised at home. This fascinating book gives beginners the chance to start making their own jewellery with the minimum of fuss. Together with a section on the basic processes that *have* to be learned, there is also detailed information on 'surface' treatments – such as etching, engraving, repoussé or chasing – and on the various stones themselves and how to mount them.

*Many more titles available and in preparation*

These and other Pan books are obtainable from all booksellers and newsagents. If you have any difficulty please send purchase price plus 7p postage to

PO Box 11  Falmouth  Cornwall